The Thinking Heart

Also by David Grossman

FICTION

More Than I Love My Life

A Horse Walks into a Bar

Falling Out of Time

To the End of the Land

Her Body Knows

Someone to Run With

Be My Knife

The Zigzag Kid

The Book of Intimate Grammar

See Under: Love

The Smile of the Lamb

NON-FICTION

Writing in the Dark:
Essays on Literature and Politics

Death as a Way of Life: Israel Ten Years After Oslo

Sleeping on a Wire: Conversations with
Palestinians in Israel

The Yellow Wind

The Thinking Heart

DAVID GROSSMAN

Essays selected by Eva Cossee and
Christoph Buchwald

Translated by Jessica Cohen

JONATHAN CAPE
LONDON

5 7 9 10 8 6

Jonathan Cape, an imprint of Vintage, is part of the
Penguin Random House group of companies
Vintage, Penguin Random House UK, One Embassy Gardens,
8 Viaduct Gardens, London SW11 7BW

penguin.co.uk/vintage
global.penguinrandomhouse.co.uk

First published by Jonathan Cape in 2024

Typeset in 11.75/14pt Garamond MT Std by Jouve (UK), Milton Keynes
Printed and bound in Great Britain by Clays Ltd, Elcograf S.p.A.

The authorised representative in the EEA is Penguin Random House Ireland,
Morrison Chambers, 32 Nassau Street, Dublin D02 YH68

A CIP catalogue record for this book is available from the British Library

ISBN 9781787335509

Penguin Random House is committed to a sustainable future
for our business, our readers and our planet. This book is made
from Forest Stewardship Council® certified paper.

Contents

Preface I

Prologue: Who will we be when we rise from the ashes? (10 October 2023) 7

PART ONE

Nevertheless (22 May 2021) 15

Israel in chaos (30 December 2022) 21

Dictatorship threatens Israel (25 March 2023) 25

What is a Jewish state? (26 April 2023) 33

The march on Jerusalem (25 July 2023) 45

The tightrope walker looks down
(29 August 2023) 49

PART TWO

Writer in an occupying country (15 July 2017) 55

Equality is not a prize (4 August 2018) 67

The thinking heart (29 November 2022) 73

After the war (1 March 2024) 79

Suddenly a cry flew (Tel Aviv, 24 June 2024) 89

Acknowledgements 95

Preface

Every time a US president proclaims his country's support for 'Israel's right to exist', I feel a certain outrage: the statement is well-meaning, but could we imagine a president making a similar declaration about France's right to exist? Or Italy's, Holland's, Egypt's, India's? Of all the countries in the world, Israel alone finds itself in this absurd predicament. Seventy-six years of sovereignty, and Israel's existence has yet to be 'legitimised' by the rest of the world. This seems all the more inconceivable when we consider that the very nation that was almost annihilated in the Holocaust is once again living – in its own perception and that of many other nations – on the precipice.

Slogans such as 'Death to Israel' and 'Palestine from the river to the sea', now commonly heard all over the world at mass protests, on university campuses and in editorials, indicate that what lies over this precipice is not only a sometimes-just criticism of Israel by its detractors, but a refusal to 'grant' it what every other state is given: a complete, definitive, stable existence.

In the collective consciousness of many peoples, religions and states, the strange and tenuous Jewish–Israeli existence is conditional. The essays in this collection explore whether, and to what extent, such existential doubt has also permeated the minds of Jewish Israelis themselves, and how they might be affected by the 7 October massacre. One thing is clear: 'Life on the end line', as the Israeli poet Nathan Alterman phrased it, has become all the more concrete, more fragile and precarious.

The expressions I see on my fellow Israelis' faces, the heavy sighs they emit when asked simply, 'How are you?' – sighs that seem to have been held in with great effort until this seemingly trivial question punctured them – are symptoms of the current situation: nothing is trivial anymore. Everything reverberates deep down, the proximity to death that we all experienced has left us more exposed. Our sadness is no longer an 'ordinary' sadness: it is the sound of our dire understanding that there is not, and perhaps never will be, any relief, any solution to the anxiety and despair that accompany our lives here. Should we in fact despair? Should we stop striving for a solution? Do we have that privilege? May we stop turning over every stone in our search for the slimmest of chances?

Another vital truth that we Israelis have come to understand after so many months of war is that we need committed, strong allies here in the Middle East, because what we have discovered – contrary to everything we believed in, to all the arrogant illusions we were fed for decades – is that we will probably not be able to win the next war on our own.

Resigned to the inevitable, I write these words: 'the next war'.

Because even if Israel is able – with support from a few powerful states – to deal a severe blow to its enemies, it will itself suffer severe and perhaps fatal blows inflicted by a deadly coalition of Hezbollah, Hamas, the Houthis in Yemen, and perhaps ISIS. Even the IDF will not be able to withstand a simultaneous attack by several states – including Iran – on several fronts.

These assumptions lead to a number of conclusions: Israel must achieve stability and acceptance with its neighbours as quickly as possible. In other words, Israel must strive immediately for peaceful relations with those of its neighbours who are willing. Yes, this includes Iran, even if the prospects for that are slim. Peace is the foremost national priority for Israel, as it is for many Arab states. Peace must be the primary element in Israel's security policy, for it is a condition no less critical to the state's survival than its military might. Any agreement that strengthens

Israel's ties in the region – the 'Abraham Accords', for example – must address the Palestinian nation, its tragedy, and its wounds: the wound of being refugees, the wound of occupation.

The words I write here are reiterated in the pages of this book more than once, and I shall keep repeating them. They are at the heart of the conflict. Without them, we would have only a 'peace of the wealthy' that is bound to blow up in the faces of those who would ignore reality. In other words, when Israel takes any step toward peace, it does so not 'for the Palestinians', but rather, to improve its own condition and increase its chances of living a full, secure life in this fickle, violent Middle East.

Yet there are other troubling questions raised by the history of these dramatis personae – primarily, Israel and Palestine – and their relations. Is there a chance for true peace between nations that are becoming more and more religious, fanatical and nationalistic? Are they willing to genuinely relinquish the totalitarian nature of their faiths, or will they merely suspend it for a few years, until they can accumulate enough military power to launch a surprise attack on their neighbour?

These are trenchant questions that must be considered honestly and comprehensively. Today, after 7 October, I can answer them only by way of negation: if the situation between Israel and its neighbours does not fundamentally shift, and if we find ourselves mired in a war as deadly as the current one every few years, Israel and Palestine will become nations whose entire being is war and hatred, nationalism and racism. Democracy will then be nothing more than a naïve hope. Are these the states in which we want to live and raise our children?

The essays collected here chronicle the thoughts and emotions of one person whose entire life has been spent in and between wars. A person who has never known a single day of full, stable peace in his country, and perhaps that is precisely why he has spent many decades fighting for peace.

As I write these words, tens of thousands of civilians in Israel and Lebanon are sitting in bomb shelters, while Israel and Hezbollah wage war in the skies above us. At the same time, Gaza lies in ruins, and the loss of life and displacement goes on.

Amid all this noise, both military and emotional, I have tried to give voice to the feelings and mindset imposed upon us by this endless war. This is my effort to maintain the freedom of thought cherished by every artist, every writer, through the anguish of the national conflict as well as in the moments when my own private heart is broken. There are things I might have written differently today, but I have not changed a word. I would like to believe that, at almost every junction of thought or decision, I did the right thing.

What exactly that 'right thing' is can be very difficult to pin down. Sometimes it is no more than a physical sensation: I usually trust it.

Prologue

Who will we be when we rise from the ashes?

10 October 2023

Some 1,000 killed, more than 3,000 injured, scores of people taken hostage. Every survivor is a miraculous story of resourcefulness and bravery. Countless miracles, countless acts of heroism and sacrifice by soldiers and civilians.

I look at people's faces and see shock. Numbness. Our hearts are weighed down by constant burden. Over and over again we say to each other: it's a nightmare. A nightmare beyond comparison. No words to describe it. No words to contain it.

I also see a deep sense of betrayal. The betrayal of citizens by their government – by the prime minister and his destructive coalition. A betrayal of all we hold precious as citizens, and in particular as citizens of this state. A betrayal of its formative, and binding, idea. Of the most precious deposit of all – the Jewish people's national home – which has been handed to its leaders to safeguard, and which they should have treated with reverence. But instead, what have we seen? What have we grown accustomed to seeing, as though it were inevitable? What we've seen is the utter abandonment of the state in favour of petty, greedy agendas and cynical, narrow-minded, delirious politics.

What is happening now is the concrete price Israel is paying for having been seduced for years by a corrupt leadership which drove it downhill from bad to worse; which eroded its institutions of law and justice, its military, its education system; which was willing to place it in existential danger in order to keep its prime minister out of prison.

Just think now of what we collaborated with for years. Think of all the energy, thought and money we wasted on watching Netanyahu and his family play out their Ceauşescu-style dramas. Think of the grotesque illusions they produced for our disbelieving eyes.

In the past nine months, millions of Israelis took to the streets every week to protest against the government and the man at its head. It was a movement of huge significance, an attempt to get Israel back on course, back to the lofty notion at the roots of its existence: creating a home for the Jewish people. And not just any home. Millions of Israelis wanted to build a liberal, democratic, peace-loving state that respects the faiths of all people. But instead of listening to what the protest movement had to offer, Netanyahu chose to discredit it, to depict it as traitorous, to incite against it, to deepen the hatred among

8

its factors. Yet he took every opportunity to declare how powerful Israel was, how determined, and above all – how well prepared it was to face any threat.

Tell that to the parents driven mad with grief, to the baby thrown on the side of the road. Tell that to the hostages. Tell that to the people who voted for you. Tell it to the eighty breaches in the most advanced border fence in the world.

But make no mistake, and do not be confused: with all the fury at Netanyahu and his people and his policies, the horror of these past few days was not caused by Israel. It was effected by Hamas. The occupation is a crime, but to shoot hundreds of civilians – children and parents, elderly and sick, in cold blood – that is a worse crime. Even in the hierarchy of evil, there is a 'ranking'. There is a scale of severity that common sense and natural instincts can identify. And when you see the killing fields of the music festival site, when you see Hamas terrorists on motorcycles chasing young partiers, some of whom are still dancing without realising what's going on . . .

I do not know whether Hamas operatives should be called 'animals', but they have undoubtedly lost their humanity.

We move through these nights and days like sleepwalkers. Trying to resist the temptation to watch the horrific clips and listen to the rumours. Feeling the fear seep in among those who, for the first time in fifty years – since the Yom Kippur War – are experiencing the terrifying prospect of defeat.

Who will we be when we rise from the ashes and re-enter our lives? When we viscerally feel the pain of author Haim Gouri's words, written during the 1948 Arab–Israeli war, 'How numerous are those no longer with us.' Who will we be and what kind of human beings will we be after seeing what we've seen? Where will we start after the destruction and loss of so many things we believed in and trusted?

If I may hazard a guess: Israel after the war will be much more right-wing, militant, and racist. The war forced on it will have cemented the most extreme, hateful stereotypes and prejudices that frame – and will continue to frame all the more robustly – Israeli identity. And that identity will from now on also embody the trauma of October 2023, as well as the polarisation, the internal rift.

Is it possible that what was lost – or indefinitely suspended – on 7 October was the minuscule chance for real dialogue, for each nation's true acceptance of the other's existence? And what do those who brandished the absurd notion of a 'binational state' say now? Israel and Palestine, two nations distorted and corrupted by endless war, cannot even be cousins to each other – does anyone still believe they can be conjoined twins? Many warless years will have to pass before acceptance and healing can even be considered.

In the meantime, we can only imagine the magnitude of fear and hatred that will now rise to the surface. I hope, I pray, that there will be Palestinians on the West Bank who, despite their hatred of Israel – their occupier – will set themselves apart, whether through action or words, from what their compatriots have done. As an Israeli, I have no right to preach to them or tell them what to do. But as a human being, I have a right – and an obligation – to demand of them humane and moral conduct.

Towards the end of last month, the leaders of the United States, Israel and Saudi Arabia spoke enthusiastically of a peace accord between Israel and the Saudis, which would build on Israel's normalisation agreements with Morocco and the United Arab Emirates. The Palestinians are barely present in these agreements. Netanyahu, arrogant and exuding self-confidence, managed – in his words – to sever the connection between the Palestinian problem and Israel's relations with Arab states. The Israeli–Saudi accord is not unrelated to the events of 'Black Saturday' between Gaza and Israel. The peace it would have created is a peace of the wealthy. It is an attempt to skip over the heart of the conflict. These past few days have proved that it is impossible to begin resolving the Middle Eastern tragedy without offering a solution that alleviates the Palestinians' suffering.

Are we capable of shaking off the well-worn for-
mulas and understanding that what has occurred here
is too immense and too terrible to be viewed through
stale paradigms? Even Israel's conduct and its crimes
in the occupied territories for fifty-six years cannot
justify or soften what has been laid bare: the depth of
hatred towards Israel, the painful understanding that
we Israelis will always have to live here in heightened
alertness and constant preparedness for war. In an
unceasing effort to be both Athens and Sparta at
once. And a fundamental doubt that we might ever
be able to lead a normal, free life, unfettered by
threats and anxieties. A stable, secure life. A life that
is home.

PART ONE

Nevertheless

Ha'Bima Square protest speech, Tel Aviv,
22 May 2021

*This speech was given the day after a ceasefire came
into effect following a major outbreak of Israeli–
Palestinian violence in May 2021, after protests
triggered in part by the eviction of Palestinian
families in east Jerusalem*

Good evening,

Allow me to dedicate my speech this evening to
the children of the Gaza Envelope, to the children of
the Gaza Strip, and to all children whose bodies and
souls have been scarred by this war. The eagerness of
each side to inscribe a victory upon its people's minds
has created thousands of little defeats. An entire
generation of children, in Gaza and in Ashkelon, is
growing up and will likely live forever with the trauma
of bombings, shellings and sirens. It is your minds –
the children's minds – that have truly been inscribed
by this conflict, and I feel the need to apologise for
not being able to create a better, kinder reality for
you, the sort of reality to which every child in the
world is entitled.

The latest war has illustrated, once again, the extent to which both sides, Israel and Hamas, are stuck, trapped in a lethal, vicious cycle of their own making. For decades, they have been operating like an automatic mechanism that can only repeat the same actions again and again, with ever-increasing force: another barrage of rockets, followed by more bombing, another barrage, a foray, Qasams and Iron Dome and sirens. The same familiar beat, over and over, faster and faster, fuelling itself, clouding judgement.

And then comes the moment when the war has clearly run its course, and everyone in both Israel and Gaza knows it, but they cannot stop, it cannot be stopped, as though force itself has become the end and not the means. This giant piston keeps pounding and pounding, while children in Beersheva and Gaza tremble with fear, pundits sit in TV studios showering praise on their own side and disparaging the enemy, while we – held hostage by extremists, whoever and wherever they may be – sit watching wide-eyed as human beings become targets in the 'target bank', mothers protect their children with their own bodies, apartment buildings topple, and entire families vanish in the blink of an eye.

All this might go on forever – the system has no self-cessation mechanism – unless President Biden gives the signal, at which point we will awake from the hypnotic spell of destruction, look around, and ask: What happened here? What happened *again*? Why do we feel that the most extreme parties in this conflict have once again manipulated us? And how can it be that after the hell suffered by millions of people, in Gaza and in Israel, we have not moved very far from the starting point?

I ask, not for the first time, how is it that Israel, my country, a state with enormous powers of creativity and invention and boldness, has been grinding away at this conflict for over a century and cannot seem to leverage its massive military might to alter reality? To liberate us from this curse of cyclical war? To pave a different path for us? True, it's easier to make war than peace. In fact, war needs only to be *continued*, whereas peace requires challenging, complex psychological processes which threaten nations accustomed almost exclusively to waging war.

We Israelis still refuse to acknowledge that we can no longer use force to dictate a reality that suits solely our own needs and agendas. Will this latest war finally drive home the comprehension that, at a certain point, our military might becomes almost irrelevant? That it does not matter how large and heavy the sword we carry is, because, ultimately, every sword is a double-edged one?

Now that the war has ended, the burning question is what will happen domestically – how will relations between Jews and Arabs play out? The recent events

on the streets of Israel are horrific. There is no justi-
fication for lynching people simply because they are
Jewish or Arab: that is the lowest rung of cruelty and
hatred. The victims of these attacks were murdered,
their humanity denied. The murderers became
human animals. But now – as cooler winds prevail
and the rule of law finally starts bringing the crim-
inals to justice – we can talk about what happened and
try to understand the roots of what has been exposed
in both societies. The future of both Jews and Arabs
depends on this understanding.

Israel may soon go to the polls for the fifth time in
four years. The events of May, and the magnitude of
hatred that erupted between Arabs and Jews, will
occupy a central place in the election. It is not hard
to predict how politicians will appeal to the fears
and suspicions, the racism, the lust for revenge.
The basest urges that burst into Israeli life will be the
kindling for this election campaign, and the inciters'
job will be easier than ever. All of us, I think, know
who stands to benefit. All of us also know what sort
of reality we will have here if the nationalistic, racist
extremists are calling the shots. And so the real battle
today is not between Arabs and Jews, but between
people on both sides who aspire to live in a peaceful,
fair partnership, and people – on both sides – who
feed on hatred and violence.

I hope we are able to reestablish the healthy forces

in both societies and bolster those of us who refuse to collaborate with despair. If we can do that, we will withstand the next murderous waves – which I fear will erupt periodically – and emerge with greater sobriety and maturity. That is what seems to be happening now, in the form of countless gatherings, debates, and new initiatives. By standing here today, by our determination, by our *sumud* – our perseverance toward peace, equality, and a just alliance between the two peoples – and by our 'nevertheless' attitude, which is a source of great hope in these dark days, there is a chance that we will find the path we have nearly lost: the intricate, demanding path to living here together in full equality and peace as Arabs, Jews, human beings.

Israel in chaos

30 December 2022

Everything that has happened in Israel since the election* is ostensibly a legal democratic process. But beneath the surface – as has happened more than once in history – the seeds of chaos have been sown in Israel's most vital state systems. This is not, after all, merely the enactment of new laws, extreme and outrageous though they are, but rather a profound and pivotal change, a change in our identity and in the character of the state. This change was not an election issue – this is not what Israelis voted for.

Throughout the negotiations to form a new government coalition, a verse from the book of Isaiah constantly grated on me: 'Woe unto them that call evil good, and good evil, that put darkness for light, and light for darkness, that put bitter for sweet, and sweet for bitter.' In the background, like a Chinese water torture, I constantly heard Knesset member Moshe Gafni proclaiming, 'Half the people will study

* Legislative elections on 1 November 2022 saw a right-wing coalition led by Netanyahu take control of the Knesset.

Torah and half will serve in the army.' And those words always sear my brain, in part for completely personal reasons.

The negotiations, which more closely resembled a looting spree, flickered before our eyes at high speed, in flashes of an unfamiliar, defiant logic: 'the override clause', 'the discrimination law', 'Smotrich* will be the ultimate arbiter on construction in the West Bank', 'Ben-Gvir† will be able to establish a private militia in the Occupied Territories', 'the serial criminal Aryeh Deri‡ will be able to . . .' The frenetic moves get faster and faster, with a card sharp's sleight of hand. We know someone is tricking us. Someone is pickpocketing not just our money but our future and that of our children, the existence we wanted to create here: a state where, despite all its flaws and shortcomings and blind spots, the possibility of becoming a civilised, egalitarian country with the capacity to contain contradictions and differences, one that in time would even manage to free itself of

* Bezalel Smotrich, Minister of Finance, advocate of West Bank expansion.
† Itamar Ben-Gvir, Minister of National Security and leader of the ultra-nationalist Otzma Yehudit party.
‡ Senior minister in Netanyahu's government who would be removed from his cabinet posts in 2023 due to various criminal convictions.

the cursed occupation, occasionally shines through. A state that could be Jewish, religious and secular; a democracy with an advanced high-tech industry and a traditional bent; and a beneficent home for its minorities. An Israeli state where the multiplicity of societal and human dialects would not necessarily create fears and mutual threats and racism, but would instead lead to cross-fertilisation and flourishing.

Now that the dust storm is settling, with the dimensions of the catastrophe exposed, Benjamin Netanyahu might be telling himself that after his chaos-sowing has achieved its goals – destroying the legal system, the police, education, and anything that emits a whiff of 'leftism' – he will be able to turn back the clock, erase or at least moderate the bullying, dishonest world view he himself created, and go back to acting rationally, appropriately, legally. Back to being the responsible adult in a civilised country. He is likely to discover, however, that from the place to which he has brought us, there is no return. It will be impossible to eliminate or even tame the chaos he has created. His years of turmoil have already imprinted something tangible and frightening on our reality, on the souls of the people who live in it, and on life itself.

They are here: chaos is here, with all its thirsty force. Internal hatred is here. Mutual loathing, the cruel violence on our streets, on our roads, in our schools and hospitals – they are all here. The people who call good evil and evil good are also already here. Nor is the occupation likely to end in the foreseeable future: it is already stronger than all the forces at play in the political arena. What began and was honed with great efficiency in that realm is now seeping into this one. Anarchy's gaping maw is already baring its fangs at the most fragile democracy in the Middle East.

Dictatorship threatens Israel

25 March 2023

Israel now finds itself in one of the gravest crises it has ever known. Even after the assassination of Prime Minister Yitzhak Rabin, the dangers faced by the country were less tangible: in November of 1995, it was clear that a new prime minister would be instated in a lawful, orderly transition. The situation now is different. Three of the Israeli parliament's most extreme, nationalistic members – Minister of Justice Yariv Levin; Constitution, Law and Justice Committee Chair Simcha Rothman; and Benjamin Netanyahu, the near-omnipotent prime minister – are acting with all their might and with no qualms to create a new legal system in place of the present one, which they claim discriminates against them and does not represent their world view or values.

Legally, they are within their rights: in Israel's most recent election last November, the parties that now form the ruling coalition came out four members ahead in the 120-member Knesset. But they are employing a rushed and belligerent procedure that is unprecedented in Israel. Their objective is not only to pass a series of changes to the extant system, but a total alteration of the country's DNA.

If the initiators of this so-called judicial reform are able to complete their legislative process, they will effectively revoke the rule of law in Israel. The judiciary would be subordinated to the Knesset and the government, and new judges would be appointed by politicians. In other words, the citizens of Israel would no longer be guaranteed legal protections against the arbitrariness of the regime. If the process is seen through, Israel will cease to be a democracy and will be subject to a regime that could, under certain circumstances, deteriorate into a dictatorship.

Netanyahu is embroiled in legal proceedings, having been charged with bribery, fraud and breach of trust. He has proved himself willing and able to do anything within his power to change the entire legal system in order to avoid going to prison. To that end, he has allied himself with the most messianic, thuggish, and in some cases unsavoury elements of Israeli society, and has handed critical and highly sensitive government portfolios to their representatives. Does this man have any constraints?

Netanyahu claims that his victory in the last election – which he won by a margin of 30,000 votes – entitles him to enact what he calls 'the reform'. Yet Israeli citizens did not vote to authorise such a drastic course of action. Practically speaking, the changes currently making their way through the legislative process mean that the prime minister – in this case, Netanyahu – would have the power to make whichever decisions he sees fit, with no allowance for the wishes, principles or welfare of half the nation.

Every Israeli belongs to one or another minority. Each of us might be a victim of abuse under this or that law, subject to institutionalised discrimination based on our sex, race, religion, nationality or sexual preference. And that, in part, is why hundreds of thousands of Israelis are taking to the streets every week to protest this hasty coup. They are demanding an immediate halt to the consideration of these anti-democratic laws, followed by serious and fair negotiations over the future attributes of Israel's judicial system. At the time of writing, Netanyahu and his people have refused to even slow their legislative steamroller for a second, and the protesters are also going full steam ahead: blocking highways, filling city squares, disrupting daily routines. The entire state is trapped in this chaos, with fear and worry prevailing.

The coming days will be pivotal for the country's future. All it would take is a single bullet to launch the drama into a completely different place, where members of both camps would take the law – or rather, lawlessness – into their own hands, bringing about a far more terrifying reality than the one we are currently living in. But even if this nightmarish scenario does not materialise, Israel is still in the throes of learning a tragic lesson about itself.

Where to start? Perhaps with the astonishment at how quickly most Israelis have lost their sense of power and existential security, a sense that had seemed solid to the point of arrogance, and has now dissolved into a fear that their national home – and perhaps, any day now, their private homes – will burn.

Television and radio studios are filled with pundits prophesying civil war. Right-wingers attack protesters with fists, tear gas, and even stun grenades. There have been attempts to run over protesters. Talk of 'blood on the streets' and 'the destruction of the Third Temple' is in the air, with heart-wrenching echoes of traumatic historical memories.

Can a stranger comprehend this dizzying shift from a sense of immense power to the fragility and anxiety that has suddenly gripped an entire nation? Without understanding this mechanism of the national psyche, I am not sure it is possible to decipher 'the Israeli'. And perhaps the greatest story of Israeliness today is the shattering of an illusion which all Israeli leaders worked so hard to nurture: the illusion of our miraculous national unity, that we are expected to strive for with all our being. Now that the cracks in our society have been exposed, it is also apparent how brittle and false this so-called unity

28

always was, and how hostile to one another the various constituents and their beliefs are.

For how can there be genuine unity between factions that view one another as an actual existential threat? How can there be unity if we have not truly done the national, civic work to contend with the fury, hostility and affront that have become so entrenched that the notion of splitting the country into the 'Israel' and 'Judea' of biblical times begins to sound worthy of consideration?

How can there be unity, for example, between the hundreds of thousands of settlers who have seized considerable portions of the occupied lands in the West Bank, which they view as ancestral lands that were promised to them by the Bible itself, and, conversely, those Israelis who perceive the settlers as the primary obstacle to a peace accord between Israel and the Palestinians, or, in other words – those Israelis who hold that the settlers pose the greatest threat to their children's future?

And what of the over one million ultra-Orthodox Jews who refuse to send their children to military service because, according to their faith, praying and studying Torah is what guarantees the continued existence of the Jewish people? How can there be unity, or even a reasonable partnership, between them and the Israelis whose sons and daughters are required by law to serve in the military for up to three years, some of whom sacrifice their lives for the country?

For so many years, since the State of Israel was established, the majority of Israelis have agreed to this warped arrangement, whereby religion binds itself around politics like ivy, feeds off it, and dictates to all other Israelis a way of life that is alien to them. Are we now taking the first perceptual steps toward a separation of religion and state?

There are other problems, other infected areas – the status of Israel's Arab citizens, for example – that have remained unresolved through the state's seventy-five years of existence, maintaining an impossible and near-miraculous equilibrium. After the shock waves of hostility and mutual hatred provoked by the current government, these questions may well demand real answers and force the creation of a new order, a revised contract between the disparate Israeli tribes – and between each of them and their state.

And we have barely spoken of the occupation. The leaders of the protest movement have wisely decided to suspend – at least for now – the most crucial debate around which Israeli society has been divided for fifty-five years, since Israel occupied the West Bank and the Gaza Strip. Even someone like me, who has been fighting against the occupation for over four decades, recognises – albeit sadly – that a public discussion of the occupation would simply dismantle and divide the protest movement, driving away large sectors of the public. At present, most Israelis are simply not able to look clearly at the occupation. Not yet. But I find some consolation in the fact that political and social questions which for years have stood stagnant, like swampy waters, may now be starting to move. And perhaps the prospect of rebooting the occupation question will resurface in a new, creative, bolder way, and begin to impact people's awareness.

Tectonic plates are shifting beneath our feet. I imagine that the people who are trying to hijack the country, who have the audacity to rewrite the Israeli legal system, were not expecting such widespread and zealous resistance. It seems that even the protesters, those who object to the so-called reform, are surprised at their own founts of fervour, passion, and courage. Hundreds of corporations and organisations, individuals including current and former Shin Bet and Mossad officials, tech executives, El Al pilots, and many other public and private entities, are joining the protesters' ranks every day. Thousands of reservists, who constitute the army's backbone, have announced that they will not report for duty. Even retirement-home residents in wheelchairs are out on the streets, protesting what they see as the destruction of the state they fought for.

For years, many of these activists – particularly the

youngest among them – were accused of being self-ish, cynical, spoilt, of having neither roots nor any sense of belonging to their country. And they were subjected to the worst possible accusation in Israel: being unpatriotic. But then came this great upheaval and, to everyone's astonishment, it prompted hundreds of thousands of Israelis to uncover both new and old stores of identity, values, belonging, and even to confess their love of Israel – a sentiment previously considered distasteful in some circles.

People who for decades did not fly the blue-and-white Star of David that is Israel's flag now brandish it at demonstrations, a little awkwardly but nevertheless with pride in their reclamation of what the right wing has appropriated. Many Israelis have suddenly discovered that it is possible to love their country – not with a sentimental, kitschy love, not with fascist idolatry, but rather with a clear-eyed devotion that stems from a desire to make this country our home, and a genuine aspiration to live in peace with our neighbours. This new-found emotion is rooted in a considered and mature civic-mindedness, and an understanding – now all the more profound – of the spirit of democracy, liberalism, equality and freedom.

What is a Jewish state?

26 April 2023

The answer to the complicated question in the title of this piece seems plain: the entity in which Israeli citizens – both Jews and Arabs – live today is a Jewish state. It contains a decisive Jewish majority that mostly perceives the state as the Jewish people's national home. It is largely organised by the Jewish calendar (the national day of rest is Saturday – the Jewish Sabbath; Jewish holy days and memorial days are national holidays). The dominant language is Hebrew, the language of the Bible, in which the Jewish people's identity is couched.

Countless layers of Jewish–Israeli existence have amassed over the state's seventy-five years of independence, and in fact began to form years before its establishment. They include, of course, the complex relationship between the Jewish–Israeli majority and the Arab–Israeli minority. Each moment of Israel's occurrence contains the entire DNA of the convoluted, vibrant, turbulent manifestation of the Jewish state known as the State of Israel.

*

But wait, haven't we forgotten something?

The almost complete indifference of most Israelis to the occupation of the Palestinian people and its land, an occupation that has lasted for over fifty-five years, is a substantial component in the formation of Israel's identity. To be clear: Israel does not bear sole responsibility for the absence of any true and courageous effort to resolve the conflict over the past few decades. Serious errors on the part of both the Palestinians and the Israelis have led to what now seems like a dead end. But today, as we celebrate Israel's seventy-fifth year, an occasion that invites both marvelling and reckoning, we must examine whether the term 'Jewish state' can, and may, disregard the occupation. Furthermore, we must question whether the enormity of ignoring the occupation and erasing it from Israeli consciousness can itself be disregarded.

'The situation.' That, as many readers know, is what we Israelis call our relationship with the Palestinians. It is our name for the decades-long bloodshed, the wars and 'operations' whose hunger is never sated, the occupation, the resistance to it, the construction of settlements, the trespassing – in every sense of the word – and the terrorism.

Most people who were born into 'the situation' and have lived their whole lives in it have long given up hope that it may ever be resolved. They are paralysed by its complexities: the infinite circularity, the inevitability of violence and counter-violence, the hollow slogans employed in the endless retellings of history, the way authentic human stories are turned into a manipulative 'narrative', the affront to those whose life essence is reduced to cliché.

We who were born into 'the situation' have accepted that our children and our children's children are doomed to live by the sword – and often, to die by it. We already know that might is no guarantee of victory. That every sword is a double-edged sword. We know, yet we turn a blind eye to the knowledge. We burrow deeper and deeper into ourselves and surrender to apathy and fatalism, to the consolations found in religion, to the self-aggrandisation offered by nationalism. We seek comfortable, accessible escapes, rising stars that shimmer before our glazed eyes, anything to distract us from the terrifying, destabilising questions posed by the conflict.

To those observing us, we appear increasingly passive, emotionally 'neutralised' (another horrific word in the language of conflict). But the chasm between ourselves and the reality generated by the conflict does not remain a void: it is constantly being filled by a flow of extremist, nationalistic and fundamentalist forces. These forces do everything, and stop at nothing, to impose their agenda on the frightened, paralysed majority.

It is dangerous to talk of a state's or nation's 'charac-teristics', but one can talk of acts and procedures. A clear example is what is referred to as 'the settlement enterprise', a reality-generating process that has transformed Israel. This process – geographic, polit-ical, military, and above all, psychological – was meant from the start to sabotage the chances of establishing fair, mutually accepted borders for the state, and thereby thwarted and continues to thwart a stable peace accord that would determine Israel's fate. In a similar mode, the Jewish religion itself – for decades, but primarily since the Six Day War – has wound itself around Israeli politics so tightly that it can no longer be unravelled.

Even after seventy-five years of independence, Israel has no permanent, accepted borders. Since earliest days, time after time, the state's borders have shrunk and expanded due to wars and operations, withdraw-als and occupations, and various agreements. A state that lacks agreed-upon borders exists in a perpetual, dangerous tension: between the temptation to invade its neighbours and the fear of being invaded by them. This constant tension, this existential uncertainty, makes Israel feel a little less like home and a little more like a fortress. It also determines the nature of the Jewish state today.

The Judaism I connect with is secular and humanist. It has faith in human beings. The only thing it holds sacred is human life. Those who believe in it arrive through dialogue, absolutely not through coercion.

There is a frequency in my mind on which I sense my belonging to the Jewish people, but also my occasional aversion to that belonging. I feel a powerful affinity with the Jewish people's destiny, as well as with its glorious and terrible history. With the Hebrew language in its various evolutions. With the rich culture it created. With its ironic, pained sense of humour.

The Judaism I connect with is repelled by the euphoria and arrogance I see among certain circles in today's Judaism, and by their shackled fusions that tighten around my neck: the fusing of religion with messianism, of faith with zealotry, of the national with the nationalistic and fascistic.

'The situation', which continues to metastasise, prompts a question about Israel's right to define itself as a democracy. An occupation regime cannot be democratic: it simply cannot. After all, democracy stems from the profound belief that all human beings are born equal, and that it is wrong to deny a person the right to participate in determining his or her own fate.

Years of occupation and humiliation can create the illusion that there is a hierarchy in human value. The occupied nation is eventually perceived as existentially, innately inferior. Its misery and wretchedness are perceived by the occupier as a fate that supposedly stems from its essence. (That is how, as we know, anti-Semites have always treated Jews.) Its members are viewed as people whose human rights may be denied, whose values and desires can be disparaged. It goes without saying that the occupying nation sees itself as superior and, therefore, as innate master. In this reality, and as the influence of religion grows, there is an increasing belief that it is God's will. And it is not hard to see how, in this climate, the democratic world view wanes.

And I ask: how can those who believe man is created in God's image trample that image?

It seems, at present, that thinking about the occupation and its repercussions does not arouse in most Israelis even the slightest distress, not to mention guilt, about living a life of lies and repression. Through a sophisticated set of intuitions, most Israelis have learned 'to live with it' (one is tempted to say: 'to filter it out'). Nor has thinking about the occupation done anything to spur Israeli citizens or the majority of their leaders since 1967 to take steps that could finally begin to repair the warped situation. We've grown accustomed to it. Furthermore, the State of Israel constructs its own image and the story it tells itself so efficiently and hermetically, that it has erected an impermeable barrier between its consciousness and reality.

When Jews were dispersed among seventy diasporas, they managed to incorporate a soulful yearning for the wonderful, dreamlike Eretz Yisrael (Land of Israel) into daily lives that were often marked by deprivation and persecution. That is how Benjamin III and his friend Sendrel – the fictional characters penned by Mendele Mocher Sforim in *The Travels of Benjamin III** – stand with their feet bogged down in the Diaspora while they dream of Eretz Yisrael, to which they are positive they have a claim. Very soon they will reach it, and they will fill their bellies with dates and figs, and they will find King Solomon using the legendary shamir to cut through the stones of the First Temple. 'It's all there,' says Benjamin longingly, 'there is all the places.'

This rare gift (the Fiddler on the Roof's gift) of a total belief in the power of imagination, and the ability to bargain with imagination so that it becomes reality – is manifesting again today, but this time the fiddler is on a tank, and the gift is used to erase from

---

* A satirical work on Jewish exile published in 1878.

our minds the existence of another nation, the humiliation and suffering that we inflict on it daily, and the inequities of the entire situation. This time, the gift helps us create amazingly sophisticated reality-bypass networks, which enable the nightmarish situation to persist, seemingly without us paying a price.

In other words: imagination, that metaphysical organ that played such a decisive role in fulfilling the tremendous feat of the Return to Zion, now allows those Israelis who wish to – and they are, it turns out, legion – to create for themselves a picture of reality in which an entire nation – millions of people whose homeland is here – is missing.

One of many possible answers to the question 'What is a Jewish state?' is, therefore: 'A Jewish state is a state that is skilled at living a full, intense life with a dimension of illusion and repression, engaged in a total denial of reality.'

> Imagination fans its own flames and turns to hallucination.
> Hallucination becomes matter.
> There are those who know how to mould it to their ends.
> Reality becomes hallucinatory.
> More and more people fall captive to it.
> Others are unwillingly captured by it.

But on this celebratory day, I would like to propose one more facet in the definition of a Jewish state, which, if implemented, could both strengthen Israel's Jewish identity and values, and improve its relationship with its large Palestinian minority. 'If implemented' – because at present it is not, or only in rare circumstances. But it is conceivable that one day, when the 'big' conflict between Israel and the Palestinian people is resolved, Jewish and Arab citizens of the state may find it within themselves to achieve true reconciliation as well.

Part of the great, miraculous revolution of the Jewish nation's return to its homeland is that it must now learn how to be a majority. It must heal itself from the ills of being a persecuted minority, and understand the duties of a majority toward the minorities living among it. This is not an easy exploration. It entails giving up both concrete assets and abstract ones – identity and self-perception. (Giving up stereotypes and prejudices is extremely difficult.) It requires a profound change in education curricula, for example. It requires a policy of protecting minorities from the ills of racism and hate crimes.

These steps have the power to create a reality that allows every person, from both the majority and the various minorities, to flourish, to feel protected, to feel represented in all systems of life and governance, to have equal rights and obligations, to live with dignity and parity – both economic and cultural. They may then feel valued, and able to nurture their own communities' origin stories without erasing those of others. They may heal the wounds of past injuries contained in their roots.

If these steps are taken, we will then be able to inscribe and proudly quote this verse at the entrance to the Supreme Court: 'Ye shall have one manner of law, as well for the stranger, as for the home-born' (Leviticus 24:22). And the avowed secularists among us, and the atheists, will stand at the gates of the Knesset and read with great intention, as in a secular prayer, the verse inscribed there: 'And God created man in His own image, in the image of God created He him; male and female created He them' (Genesis 1:27).

But why suffice with repairing the state's relationship with its large national minority? Why not go further and extend the aspiration to all minorities, all disadvantaged groups, of every nation, race and sex? Asylum seekers are also an anguished minority. Elderly people on the verge of hunger are suffering, too. As are disabled people, and those trapped under the poverty line, and Holocaust survivors. And more and more groups.

You may say: what you are proposing is a welfare state; what is 'Jewish' about your vision?

It is Jewish because most of these wishes, this concept of society, this world view, have already been formulated in Hebrew, in the Bible. Moreover, as I mentioned, they will now be occurring in a state in which the Jews are the majority. The term is used here not merely as a mathematical fact: for thousands of years, Jews lived as a minority of foreigners, subject to hatred and suspicion, in countries that almost always mistreated, persecuted and degraded them, and even attempted to annihilate them. Even in 'friendly' countries, the Jewish minority was in a permanent sense of instability and transience, barely tolerated by the majority. The earth constantly trembled beneath its feet, and imaginary 'cutting lines' were always marked around it.

Today, that minority is the majority, a condition that comes with a large responsibility and demands sensitivity, empathy, and an overcoming of history that I question whether we are capable of. And yet, if Israel were to implement even some of the aspirations outlined here, we could then say wholeheartedly: 'A Jewish state is the Jewish people's national home, and it views the full equality of all its citizens as its great human test, and as the realisation of its prophets' and founders' vision.'

The march on Jerusalem

25 July 2023

Tens of thousands of Israelis marched to Jerusalem over several days in July 2023 in protest at Netanyahu's plans to overhaul the judiciary and limit the powers of the Supreme Court

There were many exhilarating moments during the days and nights of the march on Jerusalem. One of them occurred on Saturday morning, when a massive human wave, quivering with thousands of blue and white flags, slowly streamed down the hillside near Shoresh and intersected with the crowds waiting at Hemed Bridge. The two camps melded together, water bottles were heaped upon the hot and weary walkers, along with slices of watermelon, ice-pops and grapes. There was generosity, goodwill and heartfelt sharing. There was the rare understanding that each of us is composed of the many people who came to this place, who continued together up the Qastel hills to Jerusalem, sweltering in the extreme heat but with their souls uplifted.

The Jewish nation has experienced rifts and divisions: Sadducees and Pharisees, Hassids and Misnagdim, and many other opposing factions. But what has been occurring in Israel these past few months is no longer on the same continuum. We do not yet have the words to adequately describe this turn of events, and that is why it is so frightening. It may transpire to have been the beginning of a process that will crumble – and possibly resolve – our society's ossified, dangerous points, but for now it is bringing to the surface Israel's secrets and lies, the cumulative historical offences, the lack of compassion, the injustices, all of which have become an intolerable dissonance that breeds mutual revulsion.

The resistance movement has also revealed how sophisticated were the mechanisms of self-deception, delusion and brainwashing in which we engaged so that, for seventy-five years, we could prevent all these hostilities from erupting. How we learned to hide them, chiefly from ourselves, and found ways to whitewash them, train them, domesticate them – and ourselves. How hollow the 'unity' mantra that sated us for decades sounds today. How false the term 'cohesion' now seems, when one side all but erases the worries, anxieties, values and wishes of the other.

We stand now, defenceless, against these grating lies which have burst forth into our exposed reality. The ground falls away beneath our feet. Great fear gnaws at us.

We have never, to this day, voiced such a trenchant

acknowledgement: our existence here – an existence that, for all its flaws, is also wonderful, yearned-for, exceptional – is made possible thanks to a few hundred pilots. It is a frightening realisation. This simple, concrete fact of our reality is terrifying.

Yet rather than merely debate the legitimacy of the pilots' decision to suspend their volunteer service in the armed forces, we ought to look elsewhere for a moment. We must look to the place where we admit that our military might – namely, our existence – depends largely on these few hundred people, and that we would therefore do well to strive for peace treaties with our enemy-neighbours as soon as possible. Otherwise, we risk another war. The truth that many of us have known for years is now in plain sight: this is vital to Israel's security.

As if the awareness that has been dulled for so many years has suddenly been thrashed, we now comprehend the responsibility – no, the culpability – of the self-proclaimed agents of Jewish history who brought about the state's greatest disaster: the settlement enterprise.

This week, the fate of Israel as a democratic state will be determined. The hundreds of thousands of Israelis who left their homes under impossible circumstances did so in order to protest and sound the alarm bells, but also because they felt the need to live, however briefly, in a proper, functional, benevolent atmosphere. It is a need that should not be taken lightly. For decades, it was stolen from us. The state became a place of violence, vulgarity, pollution. The deception perpetrated by Simcha Rothman, Yariv Levin, Itamar Ben-Gvir and Benjamin Netanyahu is, ultimately, just the artist's signature in the corner of the big picture. There is a tremendous thirst to spend even a day or two in a different moral climate. In a lucid reality. In a strong breeze of hope. How refreshing it was to see that torrent slowly pouring down the hillside outside Jerusalem, composed of hundreds of thousands of Israelis from all ethnicities and all ages, supporters of different political parties, people who founded – or whose foremothers and forefathers founded – the state, and who will absolutely not give up on their dream. Because they know that if that dream is distorted and vandalised, there will quite simply be no purpose to their lives.

The tightrope walker looks down

29 August 2023

From its very beginning, Israel has been akin to a start-up. Ever since the first command in Genesis – '*Lekh lekha*' ('Go forth') – there has been a drive of innovation, of striving, of entrepreneurship, invention and creation. Israel has known hard times and existential threats, but it has always pulsated with a vibrant spirit that radiates originality, with the capacity to do the unexpected and soar to new heights in every realm.

Then came the government coup, and Israel began to lose the free and harmonious movement of a healthy body. Everything that was natural and self-evident to most of its citizens – identification with the state, the near-familial sense of belonging – is now tentative, riddled with anxiety and reluctance. While that process predates the coup, it was the coup that caused it to erupt with such force and completely alter Israel's reality.

A process of destabilisation and disintegration is currently occurring in Israel, shattering the social contract and weakening the military and the economy.

Not only has progress been halted, but there is an accelerating regression – to conservative attitudes of discrimination and racism; to the exclusion of women, LGBTQ people, and Arabs; to principled ignorance and benightedness. As often happens in a sick body, more and more afflictions demand immediate treatment. Rising to the surface of Israeli consciousness are the significance and the implications – as well as the true costs – of the disease of chronic occupation; of the aberrant relations between the secular majority on the one hand, and, on the other, both the Haredi minority and the national ultra-Orthodox sector, which wields an even greater and more extremist influence; and of the state's volatile relations with its large Palestinian minority and that population's disastrous condition. Each of these maladies is sufficient to disrupt, or even paralyse, the natural and healthy existence of the body they plague: the State of Israel.

The sixty-four Knesset members of the governing coalition and most of their voters will likely disagree with me, but even they, if their minds are not hermetically sealed, can hardly deny that Israel's sense of its own strength and its almost unlimited power are no longer immune to doubts, fissures and fears. For the first time in years, Israelis have begun to feel what weakness means. For the first time perhaps since the Yom Kippur War, we have encountered within ourselves, slowly seeping in, an existential fear. It is the fear of those whose fate is not entirely in their own hands. The fear of the weak. And even though, as a popular rabbinic precept would have it, 'The eternal nation is not afraid', it is nevertheless startling to admit that the current fear is not merely a natural reaction to an external threat – because our enemies, our destroyers, come from within. Interestingly, the people who represent – in their own eyes – the strong, confident, commanding Israeliness are precisely the ones who today evoke in Israelis a 'diasporic' sense of fear, weakness and threat.

Like a tightrope walker who suddenly looks down at his shoes, and then into the abyss, we are becoming far more aware of the fragility of our existence here; of the terror of impermanence; of the sense that the ground is falling away beneath our feet. Suddenly, nothing can be taken for granted. Not the camaraderie, not the ethos of sacrificing for the better good, not the 'people's army', not the mutual responsibility – nothing. Before our horrified eyes, the one-of-a-kind state that was created here is being emptied out of the fundamental components of its character, its particularity, its uniqueness.

Is there a way back from this place we have reached?

Those who despair in the face of the right-wing's aggression and rapacity must be reminded again and again: the protest movement is hope, it is free motion within the inertia, it is creativity, mutual responsibility, ideological courage. It is the lifeblood of a democracy. It is the last chance for us and for our children to live a life of liberty in this country. It is what must be maintained and fuelled and adhered to, and a long-term commitment must be made to rehabilitate Israel, to rebuild what is broken and to heal its heartbreak, to get it back on its feet – until we know if it survived or if, tragically, its disease has become incurable.

PART TWO

Writer in an occupying country

Honorary doctorate acceptance speech
at the Hebrew University of Jerusalem,
15 July 2017

Chairman of the board of trustees, Mr Michael Federmann; president of the university, Professor Menahem Ben-Sasson; university rector, Professor Asher Cohen; distinguished guests. Good evening to the audience, to the PhD students who today become doctors, and to your proud families. Good evening to my fellow recipients of honorary degrees, and special greetings to the recipient of the Solomon Bublick Award, Mrs Ruth Dayan.

Thank you for the great honour that you are bestowing upon my colleagues and myself. This token of esteem and recognition is very meaningful to me, in part because I am a graduate of the Hebrew University, and to this day I carry with me all the goodness I received here, from my teachers and from the spirit of the place.

Dear friends, writers often talk of the torments of writing, of 'the dreaded blank page', of waking in a cold sweat because they suddenly see the weak spots, the vulnerabilities, of a story they have been writing – sometimes for years.

I know this distressing state, but I also know the pleasures of composing, of creating an entire fictional world out of thousands of facts and details. There is a particular kind of marvel that I feel when a character I invented begins to 'overtake' me, to run ahead and pull me forward: suddenly this invented, fictional character knows more than I do about its own fate, its future, and about other characters in the story. And then, in some way that I do not fully understand, it infuses me with the materials of life, with ideas, with plot twists and insights I never knew I had.

To me, a creative work is the possibility of touching infinity. Not mathematical infinity or philosophical infinity – but rather, human infinity. Meaning, the infinite faces of a person. The infinite strings of one's heart, one's infinite knowledge and opinions, urges, illusions, greatness and narrowness, one's inventiveness and destructive forces, one's infinite configurations. Almost every idea that comes to my mind about the character I am writing opens me up to more and more possibilities: a garden of forking paths.

'To be whole, it is enough to exist,' wrote the poet Fernando Pessoa. That wonderful line pours salt on the wounds of every writer, who knows how difficult it is to translate an imagined persona into a character that contains even a particle of that Pessoan 'wholeness', of the fullness of life that exists in one single second of a living person.

It is this wholeness – made up of infinite flaws, with defects and deficiencies of both mind and body – which an author strives to achieve. This is the wish, the compulsion: to reach that alchemical point at which suddenly, through the use of inanimate matter – symbols arranged on a page in a particular order – we have created a life.

Writers, who have written characters and dissolved into them and then come back into themselves; who have come back to find themselves now composed, in part, of their characters; who know that had they not written these characters, they would not truly know themselves – these writers know the pleasures to be found in the sense of wholeness that lives inside each of us.

It is almost banal to find this impressive, yet allow me to be impressed, today, by this banality: we, each and every one of us, are full of life. We contain endless possibilities and ways of being inside life, endless ways of living it.

But perhaps it is not banal after all. Perhaps it is something we need to remind ourselves. Because look how cautiously we avoid living all this abundance, all these things summoned by our souls, our bodies, our circumstances. So quickly, at such an early age, we ossify and diminish ourselves into a single *one*, a clearly delineated being. But perhaps it is our desire to avoid facing this confusing and sometimes deceptive abundance that makes us lose some part of our selves.

Sometimes the life unlived, the life we could have lived but were unable to, or did not have the courage to, withers inside us and vanishes. And sometimes we feel it, we see it before our eyes, and it stabs us with painful sorrow, with missed opportunities, with affront and even grief. Because something, or someone, was murdered there.

It could be a passionate love we gave up in favour of tranquillity. Or choosing an unsuitable profession, in which we moulder for the rest of our lives. Or spending an entire life in the wrong gender. It could be a thousand and one choices that are not right for us, which we make because of pressures and expectations, our own fears, our desire to be loved, our surrender to the zeitgeist.

Writing is a movement of the soul against that surrender, against that avoidance of the abundance inside us. It is a subversive movement that the writer makes, primarily against himself. We might imagine it as a stubborn massage that the writer keeps administering to his cautious, rigid, inhibited mind.

For me, writing is a free, supple, easy movement

along the imaginary axes between the little boy and the old man that I was and will be, between the man and the woman that I am, between the sane and the insane. Between the Jew-in-a-concentration-camp and the commander of that camp – both of which are in me. Between the Israeli I am and the Palestinian I could have been.

I remember, for example, the difficulties I experienced when I wrote Ora, the main character in *To the End of the Land*. For two years I struggled with her, yet I was unable to know her completely. There were so many words around her, but they had no living focal point. She did not spark that living pulse without which I cannot believe in the character I am writing: I cannot be it.

Finally, I had no choice but to do what any decent citizen in my situation would do: I sat down and wrote her a simple, old-fashioned letter, with pen and paper. I asked her: what's going on, Ora? Why are you so resistant? Where have I gone wrong with you? Why won't you surrender?

Even before I had finished the letter, I understood: it was not Ora who had to submit to me, but I who had to submit to her. In other words, I had to stop resisting the possibility of Ora inside me. I had to flow into the mould of her that was waiting deep inside me. Into the possibility of a woman inside me – the possibility of this particular woman inside me. I had to be capable of allowing the particles of my soul – and of my body – to float freely, uninhibited and incautious, without narrow-minded, practical, petty self-interest, toward the powerful magnet of Ora and the femininity she projects.

And from that moment on, she practically wrote herself.

Friends, I could talk about writing for hours, but the sun will soon begin to set. The Moab Mountains behind me, at the edge of the horizon, will be painted red, and they will gradually turn paler until their outline blurs and darkness finally descends upon us.

But before darkness comes, I would like to speak about the reality of our lives here; about what we Israelis call 'the *matzav*' – the situation – a word that in Hebrew alludes to a certain stability, even stasis, and which is in fact a euphemism for more than a century of bloodshed, war, terror, occupation and deadly fear. And mostly, of fatalism and despair.

Perhaps there is no more appropriate place to talk about the '*matzav*' than here, on Mount Scopus. Because I find it difficult to gaze at this beautiful landscape in a way that is disconnected from reality, from the fact that we are looking at what is called, in conflict-ese, 'Maaleh Edumim and E-1 Zone'. That location is precisely the point at which many Israelis, including government members, aim to begin the annexation of the West Bank. Others, myself included, believe that such an act would put an end to any chance of resolving the conflict and doom us all to a life of ceaseless war.

As I stand here before you, reality seems all the more densely present, containing not only the university, with all the wisdom, knowledge, humanity and the spirit of human freedom it has amassed for almost a century, but also the 3,000 Bedouins – men, women and children, members of a tribe that has lived here for generations, who are denied their rights and citizenship, and subjected to constant abuses, the purpose of which is to remove them from this place. They are also part of the *matzav*. They, too, are our situation: our writing on the wall.

Fifty years ago almost to the day, after the end of the Six Day War, here in the Mount Scopus amphitheatre, Lieutenant General Yitzhak Rabin, the chief of staff who oversaw Israel's victory, accepted his own honorary doctorate, and his speech reverberated throughout the country.

Rabin's speech was a successful effort to construct Israelis' collective consciousness and memory. I was thirteen at the time, and I still remember the chills it sent down my back. Rabin articulated for us Israelis the sense that we had experienced a miracle, and he expressed the magnitude of the salvation. He gave the war and its results the status of a morality tale that almost exceeded the limits of reality and reason.

'When we said, "The finest to the Air Force,"' Rabin said in his speech, referring to a famous recruitment slogan, 'we did not mean only technical aspects or manual skills. We meant that in order for our pilots to be capable of defeating all the enemy's forces, from four states, in a matter of hours, they must adhere to the values of moral virtue, of human virtue.' He continued: 'The platoons that broke through enemy lines and reached their targets [. . .] were borne by moral values and spiritual reserves – not by weapons and combat techniques.'

Rabin's speech, written by Chief Education Officer Mordechai Bar-On, is illuminating. It is impassioned yet not turbulent, although those were euphoric days. God, for example, is not mentioned even once. Nor is religious faith. Even the experience of finally touching the Western Wall's stones is described not in a religious context, but rather in a historical one: in Rabin's words, 'the soldiers touched right at the heart of Jewish history'. Just imagine the prominence that would be given to faith, to sanctity, and to God, in such a speech today.

Rabin also said: 'The joy of victory seized the entire nation. Nevertheless we encounter [. . .] a peculiar phenomenon among the soldiers. They are unable to rejoice wholeheartedly, their celebrations are marred by more than a measure of sadness and astonishment . . . Perhaps the Jewish people has not been brought up to, and is not accustomed to, feeling the joy of the occupier and the victor.'

But as Rabin uttered those words, the embryonic occupation had already begun to materialise, to evolve and branch out, and it already contained the primary cells created in every occupation – cells of nationalism and racism, and in our case also a messianic zeal. There also began to sprout among us, without a doubt, 'the joy of the occupier' that Rabin wanted so badly to believe we were incapable of, and which ultimately, through a long and tortuous path, led to his assassination, twenty-eight years later.

There is, it seems, no nation immune to the intoxication of power. Nations stronger and more steadfast than ours have not been able to withstand its seductions, much less the state of a small nation that, for most of its history, was weak and persecuted, and lacked the weapons and army with which to defend itself. A nation that in those early days of June 1967, believed it was facing a real threat of annihilation, and six days later had become almost an empire.

Fifty years have gone by. Israel has evolved unrecognisably. The country's accomplishments in almost every field are enormous and should not be taken for granted, and neither should the entire story: the Jewish people's return to its homeland from seventy diasporas and the great things it has created here are among humanity's most incredible and heroic stories.

Without denying the tragedy that has been inflicted upon the Palestinians, natives of this land, the Jewish people's transition from being a people of refugees and displaced persons, survivors of a huge catastrophe, into a flourishing, vibrant, powerful state – is almost inconceivable.

In order to preserve all that we hold dear and all the goodness we have created here, we must constantly remind ourselves of what threatens our future no less than the external dangers: first and foremost, the perversion that damages the core of Israel's existence – that it is a democracy that is no longer a democracy in the fullest sense of the word. It is an illusory democracy, and might be, very soon, an illusion of democracy.

It is a democracy because it has freedom of speech, a free press, the right to vote and to be elected to the Knesset, and the rule of law and the Supreme Court. But can a country that has occupied another people for fifty years, denying its freedom, truly claim to be a democracy? Can this idiom even exist: an occupying democracy?

A hundred years of conflict. Fifty years of occupation. What do they do to a person's soul, to the spirit of a nation? To both the occupied and the occupier? I think of the creative process that I described earlier – the sense of a person's infinity, whoever that person may be. The understanding that beneath every story there is another human story. That this is human archaeology: layers upon layers of stories, each of which is true in its own way.

But a life lived in constant war when there is no genuine intent to end the war, a life of fear and suspicion and violence, is by definition a life of restriction. It restricts the soul and the mind. It is a life of crude, stereotypical perceptions, of denying another people's humanity, and consequently, of denying any *other*.

This is the sort of climate that gives rise to fanaticism, to fascism, to dictatorial tendencies. This is the climate that transforms us from human beings into a horde, a hermetic people. These are the conditions under which a civil, democratic, pluralistic society, one that draws its strength from the rule of law and an insistence on equality and human rights, begins to collapse.

Can we confidently claim that Israeli society is aware of the magnitude of that threat? Is it capable of contending with it? Are we absolutely sure that those who lead us genuinely want to contend with it?

I began with the literary, and I end with the reality of our lives. But for me they go hand in hand. We do not know, of course, who will stand here fifty years from now. We cannot know in what sort of reality this ceremony will take place, or whether it will take place at all; I hope it will. We cannot predict which problems and hopes will be the focus of that future world. To what extent, for example, will technology have changed people's souls and even their bodies? Which layers and dialects will have been added to the Hebrew language they speak, and which will have disappeared? Will they utter in their speech, right here, the word 'peace' – *shalom*? Will they do so happily, or with the pain of disappointment and missed opportunities? Will it be with the ease of the obvious? Of a routine that has become a way of life?

I do not know what sort of Israel it will be. I can only hope with all my heart that the man or woman who stands here will be able to say, with their head held high and with genuine resolve:

I am a free person. A free people. In my country, in my home, inside my soul.

Thank you.

Equality is not a prize

4 August 2018

The potential for disunion and destruction in Israel's new 'Nationality Law'* is so conspicuous that the prime minister's insistence on not revising it suggests an ulterior motive: to keep the wound of Israel's relationship with its Arab minority constantly open. Open and festering and threatening. What might this motivation derive from? Why would the government and its leader want this result? One can only guess, but perhaps it is because a minority with open wounds is more pliable, more vulnerable to manipulations, to incitement, intimidation and fracturing. To a divide-and-conquer policy.

This is how you keep a wound open: with one stroke of a single unnecessary law, Netanyahu and his cabinet pulled the rug out from under the feet of a fifth of Israel's population. And again we must

* Israel's 'nation state' Basic Law of July 2018, known as the Nationality Law, defined Israel as the nation state of the Jewish people, and reserved only for Jews the right to self-determination.

ask – why? Because they can. Because they are confident that there is no power that can stop them. Because they want the Arab citizens of Israel to live in a perpetual state of existential insecurity. To be uncertain of their future. To always remember, at any given moment, that they depend on the good – or bad – graces of the government. That they are here conditionally. That they are present, but might at any moment become absent.

The law makes one other thing very clear, too: the prime minister of Israel is determined not to end the occupation or the apartheid in the occupied territories. Quite the opposite: he intends to enhance them and expand these conditions into the State of Israel. In other words, the Nationality Law is essentially a renunciation of the chance to ever end the conflict with the Palestinians.

As for the law's 'downgrading' of Arabic in Israel: language is a world, a consciousness, an identity, a culture. It is an endless tapestry that touches upon every fibre of life. A person – a politician – would have to be unbelievably audacious and arrogant to attempt to damage and humiliate the language of another nation (even if we accept the legislature's claim that this is merely a pro forma change). Hebrew and Arabic are siblings. They have been intertwined throughout history. Millions of Jewish Israelis drank Arabic with their mothers' milk. There are not enough words in the Hebrew language to protest this injury inflicted upon its sister.

For hundreds and thousands of years, Jews were a minority in the countries they lived in, and that experience shaped the Jewish people's identity and refined its moral sensitivity. Now we Jews are a majority, which comes with enormous responsibility and brings huge challenges. The challenges are political and social, but above all they are human: we must understand that the way a majority treats its minorities is one of the greatest tests of a democracy. The Israeli government has failed this test spectacularly, and its failure reverberates around the world – the same world that we repeatedly denounce for discriminating against its Jewish minorities.

It would, therefore, be a long-lasting tragedy if the Druze citizens of Israel were to accept mere 'compensation', financial or otherwise, for the injustice inflicted upon them by the Nationality Law. The new wave of protest rising among the Druze against the law – a just protest – could be the start of a far wider development, in which the Druze will be at the forefront of a struggle for equality for all Muslim and Christian minorities in Israel.

The fact that, at the time of writing, the Druze community leaders have chosen to accept Netanyahu's compensation plan demonstrates that years of discrimination and empty promises have apparently made them forget what genuine equality feels like. In the bleak Israeli reality at present, it seems necessary to point out that equality is not some sort of 'prize' that a citizen receives from his or her state for having done certain things for it. Or even for sacrificing his or her life for it. The ultra-Orthodox Jews who refuse to serve in the army are also citizens with equal rights. Equality is the default condition of citizenship, not a product of it. It is the soil from which citizenship grows. It is also what enables the ultimate liberty: the freedom to be different, to be other, to be separate, yet still equal.

To my mind, the recent laws passed by the government are in no small part the result of the warped way of thinking created by five decades of occupation. They are the result of a sense of ethnic superiority, of an eagerness to wallow in a self-righteous, nationalistic 'us' that rejects anyone who is not 'us' – whether because they are members of a different nation, a different religion, or a different gender.

Perhaps, though, this law is actually doing us a big favour by putting an end to illusions and self-deception, by exposing to all of us, on the left and on the right, how far we have come, how low Israel has sunk. Perhaps the Nationality Law will finally rattle all those among us, whatever our political affiliation, who fear for Israel and for its spirit, its humanity, and its Jewish, democratic and humanistic values. I have no doubt that there are a great number of these decent and clear-eyed people, who know that this law is a despicable act of betrayal by the state towards its citizens. Netanyahu, characteristically, presents the issue as a clash between left and right. But in fact this is a far more profound and critical struggle – between those who have given up, and those who still have hope. Between those who have surrendered to the nationalistic, racist seduction, and those who continue to resist it, who insist on preserving in their hearts a picture, an image, a hope, of how things might look in a proper democracy.

The thinking heart

Erasmus Prize acceptance speech,
29 November 2022

Your Majesties, Your Royal Highness, Your Excellencies, my dear friends, my beloved family, ladies and gentlemen:

Sixty-one years ago, when I was an eight-year-old boy, I had a small revelation. It happened early one morning on the number 18 bus in Jerusalem, on my way to school. The radio was on, and they were broadcasting an interview with the pianist Arthur Rubinstein. The interviewer asked: 'Mr Rubinstein, on the occasion of your seventy-fifth birthday, could you sum up your life in one line?' Without hesitation, Rubinstein replied, 'Art has made me a happy man. Thanks to art, I have known happiness.'

I remember being amazed and even a little embarrassed: in the 1950s, with the heavy shadow of the past still hanging above us, the word 'happy' was not something you were supposed to say in public. I don't think I knew a single person among my parents' circles of friends who would have dared to claim, out loud, that he or she was happy. The passengers on the bus that day, weary people who lived in my working-class neighbourhood, certainly did not enjoy the Americans' right to 'the pursuit of happiness', which I would read about years later in the US Declaration of Independence.

That incredible word, 'happiness' (in Hebrew: *osher*), rolled down the bus like a gold coin, and I – with a child's eyes – looked at the imaginary coin and I knew: I want this thing Mr Rubinstein speaks of. I want that special happiness. I want to be an artist.

More than six decades have gone by since that day, and art – writing – has brought me great happiness, much like the happiness I feel here today, with you. The happiness of being acknowledged, and even more so – of being understood. Even when writing caused me pain and suffering, it was a pain that had meaning, a suffering that stems from touching the authentic, primary materials of life. Literature – writing – taught me the pleasure of doing something subtle and precise in a coarse and murky world.

I am an absolutely secular man. I cannot believe in a God who would help me face the chaos of existence. And yet, writing has shown me the way – I'll call it the secular way – to have a horrifying sense of nothingness, of diving into loss and the total negation of life, while simultaneously experiencing a keen sense of vitality, of the fullness and positivity of life. Even after the tragedy that struck my family when we lost our son, Uri, in the war,* I learned that what allows me to withstand this duality of absence and presence – which to me is the essence of human existence – is to be immersed in the act of creation. Of art.

Ladies and gentlemen, dear friends: the theme of the Erasmus Prize this year is 'Mending a Torn World'. This term originates in an ancient Jewish notion conceived over 2,000 years ago. I do not know whether Erasmus of Rotterdam knew of it, but there is no doubt that the concept guided his way of life and mode of thinking. 'Mending the World' (in Hebrew: *tikkun olam*) describes a fundamental component of Jewish identity: an aspiration and obligation to improve our world; a sense of moral responsibility toward all people, whether Jewish or not; and a concern for social justice and even the environment.

If only I could say that the results of the recent Israeli election express these sort of humanistic, egalitarian, moral stances. They do not. Nevertheless, I remind myself again and again that there are still many people in Israel for whom despair is not an option. For whom apathy or escapism are luxuries they cannot afford and do not want. We are still here. Our parties might have lost, but our values and beliefs

* The Israel–Hezbollah War in northern Israel, Lebanon and the Golan Heights in summer 2006.

were not defeated, and they are more crucial than ever before.

Life in the Middle East has taught me to make do with little when it comes to my own wishes, too. Perhaps you are familiar with the anecdote about the American citizen who, during the Vietnam War, used to stand outside the White House for hours every Friday, holding a sign protesting the war. One day, a journalist went up to him and asked, with a sardonic smile, 'Do you really think you're going to change the world if you keep standing here?' 'Change the world?' the man replied with surprise, 'I have no intention of changing the world. I'm just making sure the world doesn't change me.'

As someone who has spent his entire life in a disaster zone – again, the Middle East – I know how easy it is to give in to 'the world': to cynicism, apathy, despair. And from there, it is a short path to religious fanaticism, nationalism, fascism.

When I search for a mind that is truly free, a person who might serve as a role model for my struggle against despair, I think of the courageous, soul-baring Jewish Dutchwoman who lived here in Amsterdam during the Second World War and the Holocaust: Etty Hillesum willingly entered the Westerbork concentration camp, and was eventually murdered at Auschwitz. Hillesum, as you know, managed to remain a free woman even under the harshest enslavement, and her entire being was a movement of the soul against the gravitational pull of despair. This is what she wrote in her diary:

> At night, as I lay in the camp on my plank bed, surrounded by women and girls gently snoring, dreaming aloud, quietly sobbing and tossing and turning, women and girls who often told me during the day, 'We don't want to think, we don't want to feel, otherwise we are sure to go out of our minds,' I was sometimes filled with an infinite tenderness . . . and I prayed, 'Let me be the thinking heart of these barracks.' [. . .] The thinking heart of a whole concentration camp.*

All of us, each of you sitting here in this auditorium, are living under far better conditions than those in which Etty Hillesum wrote those lines. Yet still, we all know that at any moment we may find that our freedom is taken away and we are surrounded by arbitrariness and tyranny, by the ills of racism, nationalism, fanaticism, by barbaric and thuggish behaviour, like the conduct of Russia toward Ukraine – a belligerence that is currently jeopardising the world's security.

* Etty Hillesum, *An Interrupted Life*, translated by Arnold J. Pomerans, Picador, 1996.

If such a moment arrives, if – under circumstances we may have trouble imagining now – the world ever turns upside down on us, as it has for millions of Ukrainians not too far from here, will we remember, will we persist in this private, heroic rebellion – to not stop being the feeling heart, the open, bared heart? And to not stop thinking?

To be the thinking heart. Again and again, the thinking heart.

Thank you.

After the war

1 March 2024

As the morning of Saturday 7 October recedes into the distance, its horrors only seem to be growing. Again and again we tell ourselves what has become the formative story of our identity and our destiny. How for several hours, thousands of Hamas terrorists invaded the homes of innocent Israeli civilians, murdered some 1,400 of them, raped and kidnapped, looted and burned. During those nightmarish hours, before the Israeli army snapped out of its shock, Israelis had a harsh and concrete glimpse of what might happen if their country not only suffered a punishing blow, but actually ceased to exist. If Israel were no longer.

I have talked with Jewish people living outside of Israel who have also said that their physical – and spiritual – existence felt shaky and vulnerable during those hours. But more than that: something of their life force had been taken, and was now lost.

Much too slowly, the army regained its wits and began to strike back. The State of Israel was still licking its wounds, but civic society was already enlisting en masse in rescue and organisation operations, with hundreds of thousands of citizens volunteering to do what the government should have been doing, were it not in a state of feckless paralysis.

At the time of writing (mid-February 2024), according to data from the Hamas-run Gaza Ministry of Health, approximately 30,000 people have been killed in the Gaza Strip since that day. They include many children and civilians, some of whom were not Hamas members and played no part in the cycle of war. 'Uninvolved', as Israel calls them in conflict-ese – the language with which nations at war deceive themselves so as not to face the repercussions of their acts.

The renowned Kabbalah scholar Gershom Scholem coined a saying: 'All the blood flows to the wound.' Four and a half months after the massacre, that is how Israel feels. The fear, the shock, the fury, the grief and humiliation and vengefulness, the mental energies of an entire nation – all of those have not stopped flowing to that wound, to the abyss into which we are still falling.

We cannot put aside our thoughts of the young girls and women, and the men, who were raped by attackers from Gaza who filmed their own crimes and broadcast them live to the victims' families; of the babies killed; of the families burned alive.

And the hostages. Those Israelis who for 151 days have been held in tunnels, some in iron cages. They are children and elderly people, women and men, who are ailing and dying of insufficient oxygen and medication, and of hopelessness. Or perhaps they are dying because ordinary human beings who are exposed to absolute, demonic evil often lose the innate will to live – the will to live in a world in which such evil and cruelty are possible. In which people like those Hamas terrorists live.

The enormity of the 7 October events sometimes erases our memory of what came before. And yet alarming cracks were appearing in Israeli society some nine months before the massacre. The government, with Benjamin Netanyahu at its head, was ramming through a series of legislative steps designed to severely weaken the Supreme Court's authority, thereby dealing a lethal blow to Israel's democratic character. Hundreds of thousands of citizens took to the streets every week, all those months ago, to protest the government's plan. The Israeli right wing supported the government. The entire nation was becoming increasingly extremist and polarised. What was once a legitimate ideological argument between right and left had evolved into a spectacle of profound hatred between the various 'tribes'. Public discourse had turned violent and toxic. And the Israeli public felt that the foundations of its national home were unstable.

For those of you who live in countries in which the concept of 'home' is taken for granted, I should explain that for me, through my Israeli lens, the word 'home' means a feeling of security, defence and belonging that envelops one's mind in warmth. Home is a place where I can exist with ease. And it is a place whose borders are acknowledged by everyone – in particular, by my neighbours.

But all these are, for me, engulfed in a yearning for something that has never been fully achieved. At present, I fear that Israel is more fortress than home. It offers neither security nor ease, and my neighbours harbour many doubts and demands of its rooms and its walls, and in some cases – of its very existence. On that awful 'Black Saturday', it turned out that not only is Israel still far from being a home in the full sense of the word, but it does not even know how to be a true fortress.

Nevertheless, Israelis are justifiably proud of the swift and efficient way they rally to offer mutual support when the country is threatened, whether by a pandemic like Covid-19, or a war. All over the world, reserve duty soldiers got on planes to join their fellow soldiers who had already been called up. They were going 'to protect our home', as they often said in interviews. There was something moving in this unique story: these young men rushed to the front from wherever they were, to protect their parents and grandparents. And they were prepared to give their lives. Equally stirring was the sense of unity that prevailed in the soldiers' tents, where political opinions were not important. All that mattered was mutual aid and comradeship.

But Israelis of my generation, who have been through many wars, are already asking, as we always do after a war: why does this unity only emerge in times of crisis? Why is it that only threats and dangers make us cohesive and bring out the best in us, and also extricate us from our strange attraction to self-destruction – to destroying our own home?

These questions provoke a painful insight: the profound despair felt by most Israelis after the massacre might be the result of 'the Jewish condition' into which we have once again been thrown. It is the condition of a persecuted, unprotected nation. A nation that, despite its enormous accomplishments in so many realms, is still, deep down inside, a nation of refugees, permeated with the prospect of being uprooted even after almost seventy-six years of sovereignty. Today it is clearer than ever that we will always have to stand guard over this penetrable, fragile home. What has also been clarified is how deeply rooted the hatred of this nation is.

Another thought follows, about these two tortured peoples: the trauma of becoming refugees is fundamental and primal for both Israelis and Palestinians, and yet neither nation is capable of viewing the other's tragedy with a shred of understanding – not to mention, compassion.

One more shameful phenomenon has come to the surface as a result of the war: Israel is the only country in the world whose elimination can openly be called for.

In demonstrations attended by hundreds of thousands, on the campuses of the world's most respected universities, on social media and in mosques all over the world, Israel's right to exist is often enthusiastically contested. Reasonable political criticism that takes into account the complexity of the situation gives way – when it comes to Israel – to a strident rhetoric of hatred that can only be cooled (if at all) by the destruction of the State of Israel. For instance, when Saddam Hussein murdered thousands of Kurds with chemical weapons, there were no calls to demolish Iraq, to wipe it off the face of the earth. Only when it comes to Israel is it permissible to publicly demand the actual elimination of a state.

Protesters, op-ed writers and public leaders must ask themselves what it is about Israel that provokes this loathing. Why is Israel – of the planet's 195 countries – alone in being conditional, as if its existence depended on the goodwill of the other nations of the world?

It is sickening to think that this murderous hatred is directed solely at a nation that not many years ago was, in fact, almost eradicated. There is also something galling about the tortuous and cynical connection between Jewish existential anxiety and the desire – prevalent among many nations and religions – that Israel cease to exist. It is, furthermore, intolerable that certain parties are attempting to force the Israeli–Palestinian conflict into a colonialist discourse. And then there are those who wilfully forget that Jews do not have another country – which would be an essential element in defining a nation or state as colonialist – and obscure the fact that Jews are not a foreign occupier in the Land of Israel; that their powerful affinity with this land is almost 4,000 years old; that this is where they emerged as a nation, a religion, a culture and a language.

One can imagine the malicious glee with which these people step on the Jewish nation's most brittle spot, on its sense of being an outsider, on its existential loneliness – that spot in which it has no refuge. It is this spot that frequently dooms it to make such fateful and destructive mistakes – destructive for both its enemies and itself.

Who will we be – Israelis, and Gazans – when this long, cruel war comes to an end? Not only will the memory of the atrocities inflicted by the two nations upon each other stand between us for many years, but, as is clear to us all, as soon as Hamas gets the chance, it will swiftly implement the goal clearly stated in its charter, namely, the religious duty to destroy Israel.

How, then, can we sign a peace treaty with such an enemy?

And yet, what choice do we have?

The Palestinians will hold their own reckoning. I, as an Israeli, ask what sort of people we will be when the war ends. Where will we direct our guilt – if we are courageous enough to feel it – for what we have inflicted upon innocent Palestinians? For the thousands of children we have killed. For the families we have destroyed.

And how will we learn – so that we are never again surprised – to live a full life on the knife's edge? But who, in fact, wants to live their life and raise their children on this knife's edge? And what price will we pay for living in constant watchfulness and suspicion, in perpetual fear? Who among us will decide that they do not want to – or cannot – live the life of an eternal soldier, a Spartan?

Who will stay here, in Israel, and will those who remain be the most extreme, the most fanatically religious, nationalistic, racist? Are we doomed to watch as the bold, creative, unique Israeliness is gradually absorbed into the tragic wound of Judaism?

These questions will likely accompany Israel for

years. There is, however, the possibility that a radically different reality will rise up to contend with them. Perhaps the recognition that this war cannot be won and, furthermore, that we cannot sustain the occupation indefinitely, will force both sides to accept the two-state solution, which, despite its drawbacks and risks (first and foremost, that Hamas will take over Palestine in a democratic election) is still the only feasible one?

This is also the time for those states that can exert influence over the two nations to use that influence. This is not the time for petty politics and cynical diplomacy. This is a rare moment when a shock wave like the one we experienced on 7 October has the power to reshape reality. Do the countries with a stake in the conflict not see that Israelis and Palestinians are no longer capable of saving themselves?

The next few months will determine the fate of two peoples. We will find out if the conflict that extends back more than a century is ripe for a reasonable, moral, human resolution.

How tragic that this will occur – if indeed it does – not from hope and enthusiasm, but from exhaustion and despair. Then again, that is the state of mind that often leads enemies to reconcile, and today it is all we can hope for. And so we shall make do with it. It seems we had to go through hell itself in order to get to the place from which one can see, on an exceptionally bright day, the distant edge of heaven.

Suddenly a cry flew

Tel Aviv, 24 June 2024

Suddenly a cry flew
out of nowhere, like the lash of a whip,
piercing and sharp,
waking us from a troubled sleep –
furious –
'Tell me, have you all gone mad?
Giving up on all this?
Just like that, despairing already,
Without a real fight?'

'Leave us alone,' we said.
'Let us withdraw into our heads
to mourn our dead
until this thing passes away
that no words can portray.
We are like mutes beneath the weight of its pain,
before the atrocity of our hostages.

'So let us be, just be,
without understanding, without thinking,
until our looted land, our trampled land,

our raped land
stops hurting.'

For a moment the lights flailed.
For a moment the tunnels wailed.
The world was black and white.
The world was coal and ice.
In the middle of the night we got up to flee,
my wife, my son, and me.
I bore the cry on one shoulder
and the hope on the other,
numbed and put under.

'How much more can we go on like this?'
my wife whispered,
so that the boy wouldn't hear
and be struck by fear.
'Our high-tech filled the world with awe
we were the start-up nation –
but it turns out we had a flaw,
we were just the warm-up band
for the guy in the crowd with a gun in his hand
who said his bullets were blanks.

'Look,' whispered my wife.
'This is how it happens.
This is what it looks like when it actually happens.'

We saw –
We saw long, silent convoys
streaming from the mountains into the valleys
and swallowed by ships that were swallowed by seas.

'It's as if in a single day of atrocities this land became
too demanding, too much for us to handle,' my wife
    said in astonishment.

'No, no,' scoffed a young man
passing by on a scooter,
with a gun in his holster, a shooter.
'No, no, it's that it took only a single day of fear
to extinguish – to rob you of –
maybe you never had it –
the desire for a land of your own.'

'It's not that we're running away,'
I said to my wife.
'We're just changing the arrangement of our elements,
We're just relocating, *inward* –'

Suddenly the boy spoke:
'*Yallah*, rise from the ashes,
from your school of fear and despair!'
So said our son,
as he grew stronger before our eyes.

He showed us pictures from an album we did not recognise
of a bloodied childhood, a war childhood, a ruined cradle,
images of a confiscated childhood.

'Because if we do not rise from the ashes now,'
the boy said, 'we will never rise again.'
'Or we will rise so different,' my wife said,
'so strange and terrible, so hard and bitter –
foes –
until finally we will no longer be those
they would be foolish to tangle with.'

'This is the last minute,' the boy roared,
'And even if it sounds trite,
for right now it is right,
because right now rules are being written.
Those who were left behind are leaving,
those who were deserted are deserting.
Speak to me, Father,
give me breath.
I'm nearly done for, Father, I'm nearing death.
My soul is weary of the call-ups, weary,
give me a hope, give me a reason –

'You are silent, Father,
so I will speak for you:
Men, women, now is the time to fight,
to go out into the streets at night.

There is whom to fight for
and there is what to fight for,
because a gift like this, a gift from life,
we will never be given again.
No other state will sprout from this strife.
It all now depends on you.
This is the time to rise, to live,
To be a nation or not to be –
To be a human or not to be –
There is for whom and there is for what –
And everything is suspended
over nothingness.'

(Translated by Leon Wieseltier)

Acknowledgements

The following pieces first appeared in the publications listed below:

'Who will we be when we rise from the ashes?': *Financial Times*, 10 October 2023

'Nevertheless': *Libération*, 22 May 2021

'Israel in chaos': *Haaretz*, 30 December 2022

'Dictatorship threatens Israel': *Atlantic*, 25 March 2023

'What is a Jewish state?': *A Jewish State: 75 Perspectives* (Academic Studies Press, 2024) / The Jewish People Policy Institute

'The march on Jerusalem': *Guardian*, 25 July 2023

'The tightrope walker looks down': *Haaretz*, 29 August 2023

'Equality is not a prize': *Haaretz*, 4 August 2018

'After the war': *New York Times*, 1 March 2024

'Suddenly a cry flew': *Liberties*, 24 June 2024